50 American Cake Recipes

By: Kelly Johnson

Table of Contents

- Red Velvet Cake
- Hummingbird Cake
- Devil's Food Cake
- Angel Food Cake
- Carrot Cake
- Pineapple Upside-Down Cake
- German Chocolate Cake
- Yellow Butter Cake
- Chocolate Fudge Cake
- Boston Cream Pie
- Coca-Cola Cake
- Texas Sheet Cake
- Pound Cake
- Lemon Poppy Seed Cake
- Funfetti Cake
- Coconut Layer Cake
- Chocolate Mayonnaise Cake

- Mississippi Mud Cake
- Peanut Butter Cake
- White Cake
- Strawberry Shortcake
- Apple Spice Cake
- Banana Cake
- Marble Cake
- Tres Leches Cake
- Butter Pecan Cake
- Oatmeal Cake
- Orange Creamsicle Cake
- Snickerdoodle Cake
- S'mores Cake
- Icebox Cake
- Blackout Cake
- Cherry Chip Cake
- Kentucky Butter Cake
- Molasses Cake
- Bourbon Cake

- Maple Walnut Cake
- Root Beer Float Cake
- Almond Joy Cake
- Boston Brown Bread Cake
- Blueberry Buckle
- Buttermilk Cake
- Pumpkin Spice Cake
- Chess Cake
- Crumb Cake
- Zucchini Cake
- Honey Bun Cake
- Strawberry Jell-O Poke Cake
- Toffee Crunch Cake
- Cornmeal Cake

Red Velvet Cake

Ingredients:

- 250 g flour
- 300 g sugar
- 2 eggs
- 240 ml buttermilk
- 120 ml vegetable oil
- 1 tbsp cocoa powder
- 1 tsp baking soda
- 1 tsp vanilla extract
- 1 tsp white vinegar
- Red food coloring

Instructions:
Preheat oven to 175°C (350°F).
Mix dry ingredients in one bowl. In another, whisk eggs, buttermilk, oil, vinegar, vanilla, and food coloring.
Combine wet and dry ingredients.
Divide into two greased cake pans.
Bake for 25–30 minutes.
Frost with cream cheese frosting once cooled.

Hummingbird Cake

Ingredients:

- 300 g flour
- 200 g sugar
- 1 tsp baking soda
- 1 tsp cinnamon
- 3 eggs
- 180 ml oil
- 1 tsp vanilla extract
- 1 can (approx. 400 g) crushed pineapple with juice
- 2 bananas, mashed
- 100 g chopped pecans

Instructions:
Preheat oven to 175°C (350°F).
Mix dry ingredients. In another bowl, combine eggs, oil, vanilla, pineapple, bananas, and nuts.
Mix wet into dry.
Pour into two greased pans.
Bake 25–30 minutes.
Frost with cream cheese frosting.

Devil's Food Cake

Ingredients:

- 225 g flour
- 75 g cocoa powder
- 1 ½ tsp baking soda
- ½ tsp salt
- 250 g sugar
- 2 eggs
- 120 ml oil
- 240 ml buttermilk
- 1 tsp vanilla extract
- 240 ml hot water

Instructions:
Preheat oven to 175°C (350°F).
Mix dry ingredients.
In another bowl, mix sugar, eggs, oil, buttermilk, and vanilla.
Combine all and add hot water last.
Pour into pans and bake 30–35 minutes.
Frost with chocolate buttercream or ganache.

Angel Food Cake

Ingredients:

- 12 egg whites
- 150 g powdered sugar
- 100 g cake flour (or sifted all-purpose flour)
- 1 tsp cream of tartar
- 1 tsp vanilla extract
- ½ tsp almond extract
- ¼ tsp salt

Instructions:
Preheat oven to 165°C (325°F).
Beat egg whites with cream of tartar and salt until soft peaks.
Gradually add sugar and beat to stiff peaks.
Fold in flour gently.
Pour into ungreased angel food cake pan.
Bake 40–45 minutes. Invert to cool.

Carrot Cake

Ingredients:

- 300 g grated carrots
- 250 g flour
- 200 g sugar
- 3 eggs
- 120 ml oil
- 1 tsp baking soda
- 1 tsp cinnamon
- ½ tsp nutmeg
- 100 g walnuts or pecans (optional)

Instructions:
Preheat oven to 175°C (350°F).
Mix eggs, sugar, and oil.
Add dry ingredients, then carrots and nuts.
Pour into greased pans and bake 30–35 minutes.
Cool and frost with cream cheese frosting.

Pineapple Upside-Down Cake

Ingredients:

- 50 g butter (for topping)
- 100 g brown sugar
- Pineapple rings
- Maraschino cherries
- **Cake batter:** 125 g butter, 150 g sugar, 2 eggs, 200 g flour, 2 tsp baking powder, 120 ml milk, 1 tsp vanilla

Instructions:
Preheat oven to 175°C (350°F).
Melt butter in cake pan, sprinkle brown sugar over.
Arrange pineapple and cherries.
Make cake batter and pour over fruit.
Bake 35–40 minutes. Cool 10 min, then invert onto plate.

German Chocolate Cake

Ingredients:

- **Cake:** 175 g bittersweet chocolate, 240 ml boiling water, 250 g flour, 1 tsp baking soda, ½ tsp salt, 225 g butter, 200 g sugar, 4 eggs, 240 ml buttermilk

- **Frosting:** 400 ml evaporated milk, 200 g sugar, 3 egg yolks, 150 g butter, 1 tsp vanilla, 150 g coconut, 100 g chopped pecans

Instructions:
Melt chocolate in boiling water.
Cream butter and sugar, then add eggs.
Add melted chocolate and alternately add flour and buttermilk.
Bake at 175°C (350°F) for 30–35 minutes.
Cook frosting until thick, stir in coconut and pecans.
Cool and spread between layers and on top.

Yellow Butter Cake

Ingredients:

- 250 g flour
- 2 tsp baking powder
- ½ tsp salt
- 225 g butter
- 300 g sugar
- 4 eggs
- 1 tsp vanilla
- 240 ml whole milk

Instructions:
Cream butter and sugar.
Add eggs one at a time, then vanilla.
Mix in dry ingredients alternating with milk.
Pour into pans and bake at 175°C (350°F) for 30–35 minutes.
Frost with chocolate or vanilla buttercream.

Chocolate Fudge Cake

Ingredients:

- 250 g flour
- 200 g sugar
- 75 g cocoa powder
- 1 ½ tsp baking powder
- 1 ½ tsp baking soda
- 1 tsp salt
- 240 ml buttermilk
- 120 ml vegetable oil
- 2 eggs
- 1 tsp vanilla extract
- 240 ml boiling water

Instructions:
Preheat oven to 175°C (350°F).
Mix dry ingredients in a bowl.
Whisk in buttermilk, oil, eggs, and vanilla.
Stir in boiling water (batter will be thin).
Pour into greased pans and bake for 30–35 minutes.
Cool, then frost with chocolate ganache or buttercream.

Boston Cream Pie

Ingredients:

- **Cake:** 250 g flour, 200 g sugar, 2 tsp baking powder, ½ tsp salt, 125 g butter, 2 eggs, 240 ml milk, 1 tsp vanilla extract

- **Filling:** 500 ml milk, 2 tbsp sugar, 3 egg yolks, 2 tbsp cornstarch, 1 tsp vanilla extract

- **Topping:** 150 g dark chocolate, 100 ml cream

Instructions:
Preheat oven to 175°C (350°F).
Mix cake ingredients and bake in two 9-inch pans for 25–30 minutes.
For filling, whisk milk, sugar, egg yolks, cornstarch, and heat until thick.
Cool and spread on one layer of cake.
Top with the second cake layer.
Make ganache by heating cream and mixing with chocolate.
Pour over cake and chill.

Coca-Cola Cake

Ingredients:

- 250 g flour
- 200 g sugar
- 75 g cocoa powder
- 1 tsp baking soda
- 1 tsp salt
- 240 ml Coca-Cola
- 120 g butter
- 2 eggs
- 1 tsp vanilla extract
- **Frosting:** 100 g butter, 100 g cocoa powder, 200 g powdered sugar, 60 ml milk, 1 tsp vanilla extract

Instructions:
Preheat oven to 175°C (350°F).
Mix dry ingredients.
Add Coca-Cola, butter, eggs, and vanilla.
Pour into greased pan and bake for 30–35 minutes.
For frosting, melt butter, stir in cocoa, then add powdered sugar and milk.
Spread on warm cake.

Texas Sheet Cake

Ingredients:

- **Cake:** 250 g flour, 200 g sugar, 1 tsp baking soda, 1 tsp salt, 2 eggs, 240 ml buttermilk, 120 ml vegetable oil, 1 tsp vanilla extract, 100 g cocoa powder, 240 ml boiling water

- **Frosting:** 100 g butter, 200 g powdered sugar, 2 tbsp cocoa powder, 60 ml milk, 1 tsp vanilla extract, 50 g chopped pecans

Instructions:

Preheat oven to 175°C (350°F).
Mix dry ingredients, then add eggs, buttermilk, oil, and vanilla.
Stir in cocoa and boiling water.
Pour into a greased baking sheet.
Bake for 25–30 minutes.
For frosting, melt butter, stir in cocoa, milk, and powdered sugar, then add vanilla and pecans.
Spread over warm cake.

Pound Cake

Ingredients:

- 250 g butter
- 250 g sugar
- 4 eggs
- 250 g flour
- 1 tsp vanilla extract
- ¼ tsp salt
- 60 ml milk

Instructions:
Preheat oven to 175°C (350°F).
Cream butter and sugar.
Add eggs one at a time.
Mix in flour, salt, and vanilla.
Add milk to thin out the batter.
Pour into greased loaf pan and bake for 50–60 minutes.

Lemon Poppy Seed Cake

Ingredients:

- 250 g flour
- 200 g sugar
- 1 ½ tsp baking powder
- 1 tsp baking soda
- 3 eggs
- 240 ml vegetable oil
- 2 tbsp poppy seeds
- Zest of 2 lemons
- 240 ml buttermilk
- 1 tsp vanilla extract
- **Glaze:** 100 g powdered sugar, 2 tbsp lemon juice

Instructions:
Preheat oven to 175°C (350°F).
Mix dry ingredients.
In another bowl, whisk eggs, oil, buttermilk, lemon zest, and vanilla.
Add dry to wet ingredients, fold in poppy seeds.
Bake for 30–35 minutes.
Mix glaze and drizzle over cooled cake.

Funfetti Cake

Ingredients:

- 250 g flour
- 200 g sugar
- 1 tsp baking powder
- ½ tsp baking soda
- ½ tsp salt
- 2 eggs
- 240 ml milk
- 120 g butter, softened
- 1 tsp vanilla extract
- 100 g sprinkles (nonpareils or jimmies)

Instructions:
Preheat oven to 175°C (350°F).
Cream butter and sugar.
Add eggs and vanilla, then alternately add flour mixture and milk.
Fold in sprinkles.
Bake for 25–30 minutes.
Frost with buttercream and more sprinkles.

Coconut Layer Cake

Ingredients:

- **Cake:** 250 g flour, 200 g sugar, 1 tsp baking powder, ½ tsp salt, 240 ml coconut milk, 120 g butter, 2 eggs, 1 tsp vanilla extract, 100 g shredded coconut

- **Frosting:** 200 g butter, 300 g powdered sugar, 1 tsp vanilla extract, 240 ml coconut cream, 100 g shredded coconut

Instructions:
Preheat oven to 175°C (350°F).
Cream butter and sugar.
Add eggs, then flour, salt, and baking powder.
Add coconut milk and vanilla.
Fold in shredded coconut.
Pour into two greased pans and bake for 25–30 minutes.
For frosting, whip butter, powdered sugar, coconut cream, and vanilla.
Frost and sprinkle with coconut.

Chocolate Mayonnaise Cake

Ingredients:

- 250 g flour
- 200 g sugar
- 50 g cocoa powder
- 1 tsp baking soda
- ½ tsp salt
- 2 eggs
- 240 ml mayonnaise
- 240 ml water
- 1 tsp vanilla extract

Instructions:
Preheat oven to 175°C (350°F).
Mix dry ingredients.
Add eggs, mayonnaise, water, and vanilla.
Stir until smooth.
Pour into greased pans and bake for 30–35 minutes.
Cool and frost with chocolate ganache or buttercream.

Mississippi Mud Cake

Ingredients:

- **Cake:** 200 g sugar, 200 g butter, 50 g cocoa powder, 240 ml buttermilk, 2 eggs, 250 g flour, 1 tsp baking soda, ½ tsp salt

- **Topping:** 100 g butter, 200 g powdered sugar, 30 g cocoa powder, 60 ml milk, 1 tsp vanilla extract, 100 g chopped pecans

Instructions:
Preheat oven to 175°C (350°F).
Mix butter, sugar, cocoa, and buttermilk, then add eggs.
Add dry ingredients and mix.
Pour into greased pan and bake for 30–35 minutes.
For topping, melt butter and stir in cocoa, powdered sugar, milk, and vanilla.
Pour over cake, sprinkle with pecans, and cool.

Peanut Butter Cake

Ingredients:

- 250 g flour
- 200 g sugar
- 1 tsp baking powder
- ½ tsp baking soda
- ¼ tsp salt
- 240 g peanut butter
- 240 ml milk
- 2 eggs
- 1 tsp vanilla extract

Instructions:
Preheat oven to 175°C (350°F).
Mix dry ingredients.
Cream peanut butter, sugar, and eggs.
Add dry ingredients and milk alternately.
Pour into greased pans and bake for 25–30 minutes.
Frost with peanut butter frosting or chocolate ganache.

White Cake

Ingredients:

- 250 g flour
- 200 g sugar
- 1 tsp baking powder
- ½ tsp salt
- 240 g butter
- 3 egg whites
- 240 ml milk
- 1 tsp vanilla extract

Instructions:
Preheat oven to 175°C (350°F).
Cream butter and sugar.
Add egg whites and vanilla.
Mix in dry ingredients alternately with milk.
Pour into greased pans and bake for 25–30 minutes.
Frost with vanilla buttercream or fruit filling.

Strawberry Shortcake

Ingredients:

- **Cake:** 250 g flour, 200 g sugar, 1 tsp baking powder, ½ tsp baking soda, ¼ tsp salt, 120 g butter, 240 ml buttermilk, 1 tsp vanilla extract

- **Filling:** 500 g strawberries, 100 g sugar

- **Whipped cream:** 240 ml heavy cream, 2 tbsp sugar, 1 tsp vanilla

Instructions:
Preheat oven to 175°C (350°F).
Mix dry ingredients.
Add butter, buttermilk, and vanilla.
Pour into greased pans and bake for 25–30 minutes.
Slice strawberries and mix with sugar, then let sit.
Whip cream with sugar and vanilla.
Assemble cake by layering cake, strawberries, and whipped cream.

Apple Spice Cake

Ingredients:

- 250 g flour
- 200 g sugar
- 1 tsp cinnamon
- 1 tsp baking soda
- ½ tsp baking powder
- ½ tsp salt
- 2 eggs
- 240 g grated apples (about 2 apples)
- 120 ml vegetable oil
- 1 tsp vanilla extract

Instructions:
Preheat oven to 175°C (350°F).
Mix dry ingredients.
Whisk eggs, oil, and vanilla, then add grated apples.
Fold in dry ingredients.
Pour into greased pan and bake for 30–35 minutes.
Cool and frost with cream cheese frosting or dust with powdered sugar.

Banana Cake

Ingredients:

- 250 g flour
- 200 g sugar
- 1 tsp baking soda
- ½ tsp salt
- 2 ripe bananas, mashed
- 2 eggs
- 120 ml vegetable oil
- 1 tsp vanilla extract
- 120 ml buttermilk

Instructions:
Preheat oven to 175°C (350°F).
Mix dry ingredients.
In another bowl, combine mashed bananas, eggs, oil, vanilla, and buttermilk.
Fold wet ingredients into dry.
Pour into greased pans and bake for 25–30 minutes.
Frost with cream cheese frosting or buttercream.

Marble Cake

Ingredients:

- 250 g flour
- 200 g sugar
- 1 tsp baking powder
- ½ tsp salt
- 2 eggs
- 240 ml milk
- 120 g butter
- 1 tsp vanilla extract
- 50 g cocoa powder

Instructions:

Preheat oven to 175°C (350°F).
Cream butter and sugar, add eggs and vanilla.
Add flour, salt, and baking powder, alternating with milk.
Divide batter into two parts.
Mix cocoa powder with one part.
Spoon alternating batter into pan and swirl with a knife.
Bake for 30–35 minutes.
Cool and frost with chocolate or vanilla buttercream.

Tres Leches Cake

Ingredients:

- **Cake:** 250 g flour, 200 g sugar, 1 tsp baking powder, ¼ tsp salt, 4 eggs, 240 ml milk, 1 tsp vanilla extract

- **Milk mixture:** 120 ml evaporated milk, 120 ml sweetened condensed milk, 120 ml whole milk

- **Whipped cream:** 240 ml heavy cream, 2 tbsp powdered sugar, 1 tsp vanilla extract

Instructions:
Preheat oven to 175°C (350°F).
Mix dry ingredients.
Whisk eggs, milk, and vanilla, then add to dry ingredients.
Pour into greased pan and bake for 25–30 minutes.
Cool slightly, then poke holes and pour milk mixture over.
Chill for 2 hours.
Whip cream with powdered sugar and vanilla, then spread over cake.

Butter Pecan Cake

Ingredients:

- **Cake:** 250 g flour, 200 g sugar, 1 tsp baking powder, ½ tsp salt, 240 g butter, 2 eggs, 120 ml buttermilk, 1 tsp vanilla extract, 100 g chopped pecans

- **Frosting:** 240 g butter, 300 g powdered sugar, 1 tsp vanilla extract, 50 g chopped pecans

Instructions:
Preheat oven to 175°C (350°F).
Cream butter and sugar, then add eggs and vanilla.
Add flour, baking powder, salt, and buttermilk.
Fold in chopped pecans.
Pour into greased pans and bake for 25–30 minutes.
For frosting, whip butter, powdered sugar, and vanilla.
Frost cake and top with chopped pecans.

Oatmeal Cake

Ingredients:

- 250 g flour, 200 g sugar, 1 tsp baking soda, ½ tsp salt, 2 eggs, 240 ml milk, 120 g butter, 100 g rolled oats, 1 tsp vanilla extract

- **Topping:** 100 g butter, 100 g brown sugar, 50 g shredded coconut, 50 g chopped walnuts

Instructions:
Preheat oven to 175°C (350°F).
Mix dry ingredients.
Add eggs, milk, melted butter, oats, and vanilla, and combine.
Pour into greased pan and bake for 30–35 minutes.
For topping, melt butter, then stir in brown sugar, coconut, and walnuts.
Spread over cake and bake for an additional 5–10 minutes.

Orange Creamsicle Cake

Ingredients:

- **Cake:** 250 g flour, 200 g sugar, 1 tsp baking powder, ½ tsp baking soda, ½ tsp salt, 240 ml orange juice, 120 g butter, 2 eggs, zest of 1 orange

- **Frosting:** 240 g butter, 300 g powdered sugar, 60 ml orange juice, 1 tsp vanilla extract

Instructions:
Preheat oven to 175°C (350°F).
Cream butter and sugar, add eggs and orange zest.
Add flour, baking powder, baking soda, and salt, then stir in orange juice.
Pour into greased pans and bake for 25–30 minutes.
For frosting, beat butter, powdered sugar, orange juice, and vanilla.
Frost cake once cooled.

Snickerdoodle Cake

Ingredients:

- 250 g flour, 200 g sugar, 1 tsp baking powder, ½ tsp baking soda, 1 tsp cinnamon, ½ tsp salt, 120 g butter, 2 eggs, 240 ml buttermilk

- **Topping:** 2 tbsp sugar, 1 tsp cinnamon

Instructions:
Preheat oven to 175°C (350°F).
Cream butter and sugar, then add eggs and vanilla.
Add flour, baking powder, baking soda, cinnamon, salt, and buttermilk.
Pour into greased pan and bake for 25–30 minutes.
Mix sugar and cinnamon, then sprinkle over cake before baking.

S'mores Cake

Ingredients:

- **Cake:** 250 g flour, 200 g sugar, 1 tsp baking powder, ½ tsp salt, 50 g cocoa powder, 240 ml milk, 120 g butter, 2 eggs, 1 tsp vanilla extract, 100 g graham cracker crumbs

- **Frosting:** 240 g butter, 300 g powdered sugar, 1 tsp vanilla extract, 100 g mini marshmallows, 50 g chocolate chips

Instructions:
Preheat oven to 175°C (350°F).
Mix dry ingredients, then add eggs, milk, butter, and vanilla.
Fold in graham cracker crumbs.
Pour into greased pans and bake for 25–30 minutes.
For frosting, whip butter and powdered sugar, then stir in vanilla.
Top cake with mini marshmallows and chocolate chips, then broil briefly to melt.

Icebox Cake

Ingredients:

- **Cake:** 250 g graham crackers, 500 ml heavy cream, 100 g powdered sugar, 1 tsp vanilla extract

- **Topping:** 50 g chocolate chips, 1 tbsp butter

Instructions:
Layer graham crackers in the bottom of a pan.
Whip cream with powdered sugar and vanilla until stiff peaks form.
Spread whipped cream over graham crackers.
Repeat layers until pan is full.
Chill in the fridge for at least 4 hours or overnight.
Melt chocolate and butter together, drizzle over cake before serving.

Blackout Cake

Ingredients:

- **Cake:** 250 g flour, 200 g sugar, 1 tsp baking powder, 1 tsp baking soda, 50 g cocoa powder, 2 eggs, 240 ml milk, 120 ml vegetable oil, 1 tsp vanilla extract

- **Frosting:** 200 g dark chocolate, 100 ml cream, 100 g powdered sugar

Instructions:
Preheat oven to 175°C (350°F).
Mix dry ingredients, then add eggs, milk, oil, and vanilla.
Pour into greased pans and bake for 30–35 minutes.
For frosting, heat cream and pour over chopped chocolate.
Let sit for a few minutes, then stir until smooth.
Frost cooled cake and chill until set.

Cherry Chip Cake

Ingredients:

- **Cake:** 250 g flour, 200 g sugar, 1 tsp baking powder, ½ tsp baking soda, ½ tsp salt, 240 ml milk, 120 g butter, 2 eggs, 1 tsp vanilla extract, 100 g maraschino cherries, chopped

- **Frosting:** 240 g butter, 300 g powdered sugar, 2 tbsp maraschino cherry juice, 1 tsp vanilla extract

Instructions:
Preheat oven to 175°C (350°F).
Mix dry ingredients, then add eggs, milk, butter, and vanilla.
Fold in chopped cherries.
Pour into greased pans and bake for 25–30 minutes.
For frosting, beat butter and powdered sugar, then add cherry juice and vanilla.
Frost cooled cake and top with additional chopped cherries if desired.

Kentucky Butter Cake

Ingredients:

- **Cake:** 250 g flour, 200 g sugar, 1 tsp baking powder, ½ tsp baking soda, ¼ tsp salt, 240 g butter, 2 eggs, 240 ml buttermilk, 1 tsp vanilla extract

- **Glaze:** 120 g butter, 200 g sugar, 120 ml water, 1 tsp vanilla extract

Instructions:

Preheat oven to 175°C (350°F).
Mix dry ingredients.
Cream butter and sugar, add eggs, then alternate adding dry ingredients and buttermilk.
Pour into greased pan and bake for 30–35 minutes.
For glaze, melt butter, then stir in sugar and water.
Bring to a boil and cook for 2–3 minutes.
Pour glaze over cake while still warm and let soak.

Molasses Cake

Ingredients:

- 250 g flour, 200 g sugar, 1 tsp baking soda, 1 tsp ground ginger, ½ tsp ground cinnamon, ½ tsp ground cloves, ½ tsp salt, 120 g butter, 240 ml molasses, 2 eggs, 240 ml boiling water

Instructions:

Preheat oven to 175°C (350°F).
Cream butter and sugar, then add molasses and eggs.
Combine dry ingredients and add to wet mixture alternately with boiling water.
Pour into greased pan and bake for 25–30 minutes.
Cool and frost with cream cheese frosting if desired.

Bourbon Cake

Ingredients:

- **Cake:** 250 g flour, 200 g sugar, 1 tsp baking powder, ½ tsp baking soda, ½ tsp salt, 240 g butter, 2 eggs, 240 ml buttermilk, 2 tbsp bourbon, 1 tsp vanilla extract

- **Glaze:** 100 g butter, 100 g brown sugar, 60 ml bourbon, 1 tsp vanilla extract

Instructions:
Preheat oven to 175°C (350°F).
Mix dry ingredients.
Cream butter and sugar, then add eggs.
Alternate adding dry ingredients and buttermilk, then stir in bourbon and vanilla.
Pour into greased pan and bake for 30–35 minutes.
For glaze, melt butter, then stir in brown sugar, bourbon, and vanilla.
Pour over cake and let soak for a few minutes before serving.

Maple Walnut Cake

Ingredients:

- **Cake:** 250 g flour, 200 g sugar, 1 tsp baking powder, ½ tsp salt, 120 g butter, 2 eggs, 240 ml maple syrup, 1 tsp vanilla extract, 100 g chopped walnuts

- **Frosting:** 240 g cream cheese, 100 g powdered sugar, 60 ml maple syrup, 1 tsp vanilla extract

Instructions:
Preheat oven to 175°C (350°F).
Cream butter and sugar, then add eggs and maple syrup.
Mix in dry ingredients and fold in walnuts.
Pour into greased pan and bake for 25–30 minutes.
For frosting, beat cream cheese with powdered sugar, maple syrup, and vanilla.
Frost cooled cake.

Root Beer Float Cake

Ingredients:

- **Cake:** 250 g flour, 200 g sugar, 1 tsp baking powder, ½ tsp baking soda, 1 tsp vanilla extract, 240 ml root beer, 120 g butter, 2 eggs

- **Frosting:** 240 ml heavy cream, 100 g powdered sugar, 1 tsp vanilla extract

Instructions:
Preheat oven to 175°C (350°F).
Mix dry ingredients, then add eggs, vanilla, and root beer.
Pour into greased pan and bake for 25–30 minutes.
For frosting, beat heavy cream with powdered sugar and vanilla until stiff peaks form.
Frost cake and serve.

Almond Joy Cake

Ingredients:

- **Cake:** 250 g flour, 200 g sugar, 1 tsp baking powder, ½ tsp salt, 240 g butter, 2 eggs, 240 ml milk, 1 tsp vanilla extract, 100 g shredded coconut, 100 g chopped almonds, 100 g chocolate chips

- **Frosting:** 240 g butter, 200 g powdered sugar, 1 tsp vanilla extract, 100 g shredded coconut, 100 g chopped almonds

Instructions:

Preheat oven to 175°C (350°F).
Mix dry ingredients, then add eggs, milk, and vanilla.
Fold in coconut, almonds, and chocolate chips.
Pour into greased pan and bake for 30–35 minutes.
For frosting, beat butter and powdered sugar, then stir in vanilla, coconut, and almonds.
Frost cooled cake.

Boston Brown Bread Cake

Ingredients:

- 250 g flour, 100 g cornmeal, 1 tsp baking soda, ½ tsp salt, 240 ml buttermilk, 120 g molasses, 1 egg, 100 g raisins

Instructions:
Preheat oven to 175°C (350°F).
Mix dry ingredients.
In a separate bowl, combine buttermilk, molasses, and egg.
Add wet ingredients to dry and stir in raisins.
Pour into greased pan and bake for 30–35 minutes.
Cool and serve with butter or cream cheese.

Blueberry Buckle

Ingredients:

- **Cake:** 250 g flour, 200 g sugar, 1 tsp baking powder, ½ tsp baking soda, ½ tsp salt, 240 g butter, 2 eggs, 240 ml milk, 1 tsp vanilla extract, 200 g blueberries

- **Topping:** 100 g sugar, 50 g flour, 50 g butter, 1 tsp cinnamon

Instructions:
Preheat oven to 175°C (350°F).
Mix dry ingredients for the cake.
Cream butter and sugar, then add eggs and vanilla.
Alternate adding dry ingredients and milk.
Fold in blueberries.
Pour into greased pan and bake for 25–30 minutes.
For topping, combine sugar, flour, butter, and cinnamon, then sprinkle over cake before baking.

Buttermilk Cake

Ingredients:

- **Cake:** 250 g flour, 200 g sugar, 1 tsp baking powder, ½ tsp baking soda, ¼ tsp salt, 240 g butter, 2 eggs, 240 ml buttermilk, 1 tsp vanilla extract

- **Frosting:** 240 g powdered sugar, 60 g butter, 2 tbsp milk, 1 tsp vanilla extract

Instructions:

Preheat oven to 175°C (350°F).
Cream butter and sugar, then add eggs and vanilla.
Alternate adding dry ingredients and buttermilk.
Pour into greased pan and bake for 30–35 minutes.
For frosting, melt butter and whisk with powdered sugar, milk, and vanilla.
Frost the cake once cooled.

Pumpkin Spice Cake

Ingredients:

- **Cake:** 250 g flour, 200 g sugar, 1 tsp baking powder, 1 tsp baking soda, 1 tsp ground cinnamon, ½ tsp ground nutmeg, ½ tsp ground ginger, ¼ tsp ground cloves, ½ tsp salt, 240 g butter, 2 eggs, 240 ml canned pumpkin, 1 tsp vanilla extract

- **Frosting:** 240 g cream cheese, 100 g powdered sugar, 1 tsp vanilla extract, 60 g butter

Instructions:
Preheat oven to 175°C (350°F).
Mix dry ingredients, then cream butter and sugar.
Add eggs, then stir in pumpkin and vanilla.
Add dry ingredients alternately with butter, and mix until combined.
Pour into greased pan and bake for 25–30 minutes.
For frosting, beat cream cheese, butter, powdered sugar, and vanilla.
Frost cooled cake.

Chess Cake

Ingredients:

- **Cake:** 250 g flour, 200 g sugar, 1 tsp baking powder, ½ tsp salt, 240 g butter, 2 eggs, 240 ml milk, 1 tsp vanilla extract

- **Cream Cheese Layer:** 240 g cream cheese, 200 g powdered sugar, 1 tsp vanilla extract, 1 egg

- **Topping:** 100 g sugar, 1 tsp vanilla extract

Instructions:
Preheat oven to 175°C (350°F).
Mix dry ingredients for the cake, then cream butter and sugar.
Add eggs, milk, and vanilla.
Pour batter into greased pan.
For the cream cheese layer, beat cream cheese, powdered sugar, vanilla, and egg, then spread over the batter.
Sprinkle sugar on top.
Bake for 30–35 minutes until golden and set.

Crumb Cake

Ingredients:

- **Cake:** 250 g flour, 200 g sugar, 1 tsp baking powder, ½ tsp baking soda, ½ tsp salt, 240 g butter, 2 eggs, 240 ml buttermilk, 1 tsp vanilla extract

- **Crumb Topping:** 100 g flour, 100 g sugar, 1 tsp cinnamon, 100 g butter, melted

Instructions:
Preheat oven to 175°C (350°F).
Mix dry ingredients for the cake.
Cream butter and sugar, add eggs, then stir in vanilla and buttermilk.
Pour into greased pan.
For the crumb topping, combine flour, sugar, cinnamon, and melted butter.
Sprinkle over cake.
Bake for 25–30 minutes.

Zucchini Cake

Ingredients:

- **Cake:** 250 g flour, 200 g sugar, 1 tsp baking powder, ½ tsp baking soda, 1 tsp ground cinnamon, ½ tsp ground nutmeg, ½ tsp salt, 240 g butter, 2 eggs, 240 ml grated zucchini, 1 tsp vanilla extract

- **Frosting:** 240 g cream cheese, 100 g powdered sugar, 1 tsp vanilla extract, 60 g butter

Instructions:

Preheat oven to 175°C (350°F).
Mix dry ingredients, then cream butter and sugar.
Add eggs, then stir in zucchini and vanilla.
Add dry ingredients and mix well.
Pour into greased pan and bake for 25–30 minutes.
For frosting, beat cream cheese, butter, powdered sugar, and vanilla.
Frost cooled cake.

Honey Bun Cake

Ingredients:

- **Cake:** 250 g flour, 200 g sugar, 1 tsp baking powder, 1 tsp baking soda, ½ tsp salt, 240 g butter, 2 eggs, 240 ml sour cream, 1 tsp vanilla extract

- **Cinnamon Swirl:** 100 g brown sugar, 1 tbsp cinnamon

- **Glaze:** 200 g powdered sugar, 2 tbsp milk, 1 tsp vanilla extract

Instructions:
Preheat oven to 175°C (350°F).
Mix dry ingredients for the cake, then cream butter and sugar.
Add eggs, sour cream, and vanilla.
In a separate bowl, combine cinnamon and brown sugar for the swirl.
Pour half the batter into a greased pan, then sprinkle with cinnamon mixture.
Top with the remaining batter and swirl.
Bake for 30–35 minutes.
For the glaze, whisk powdered sugar, milk, and vanilla, then drizzle over the cake.

Strawberry Jell-O Poke Cake

Ingredients:

- **Cake:** 250 g flour, 200 g sugar, 1 tsp baking powder, ½ tsp salt, 240 g butter, 2 eggs, 240 ml milk, 1 tsp vanilla extract

- **Jell-O Layer:** 1 package strawberry Jell-O, 240 ml boiling water

- **Frosting:** 240 ml heavy cream, 100 g powdered sugar, 1 tsp vanilla extract

Instructions:

Preheat oven to 175°C (350°F).
Mix dry ingredients, then cream butter and sugar.
Add eggs and milk, then vanilla.
Pour into greased pan and bake for 25–30 minutes.
While the cake is baking, prepare the Jell-O by dissolving it in boiling water.
Once the cake is done, poke holes all over it and pour the Jell-O over the cake.
Chill in the fridge.
For frosting, beat heavy cream, powdered sugar, and vanilla until stiff peaks form.
Frost cake after it has chilled.

Toffee Crunch Cake

Ingredients:

- **Cake:** 250 g flour, 200 g sugar, 1 tsp baking powder, ½ tsp baking soda, ½ tsp salt, 240 g butter, 2 eggs, 240 ml buttermilk, 1 tsp vanilla extract, 100 g toffee bits

- **Frosting:** 240 g butter, 200 g powdered sugar, 1 tsp vanilla extract, 60 g toffee bits

Instructions:
Preheat oven to 175°C (350°F).
Mix dry ingredients, then cream butter and sugar.
Add eggs, buttermilk, and vanilla.
Fold in toffee bits.
Pour into greased pan and bake for 30–35 minutes.
For frosting, beat butter and powdered sugar, then stir in vanilla.
Frost the cake and top with additional toffee bits.

Cornmeal Cake

Ingredients:

- **Cake:** 250 g cornmeal, 200 g flour, 200 g sugar, 1 tsp baking powder, 1 tsp salt, 240 g butter, 2 eggs, 240 ml milk, 1 tsp vanilla extract

- **Frosting:** 240 g butter, 200 g powdered sugar, 1 tsp vanilla extract

Instructions:
Preheat oven to 175°C (350°F).
Mix dry ingredients.
Cream butter and sugar, then add eggs, milk, and vanilla.
Add dry ingredients and mix well.
Pour into greased pan and bake for 30–35 minutes.
For frosting, beat butter and powdered sugar with vanilla.
Frost cooled cake.

www.ingramcontent.com/pod-product-compliance
Lightning Source LLC
LaVergne TN
LVHW081323060526
838201LV00055B/2419